C00 740 098X

D0537294

WONDERS
of the
WORLD

Artist and author:

Mark Bergin was born in Hastings, England, in 1961. He studied at Eastbourne College of Art and has specialised in historical reconstructions, aviation and maritime subjects since 1983. He has been commissioned by aerospace companies and has illustrated a number of books on flight. He has also illustrated many books in the prize-winning *Inside Story* series. He lives in Bexhill-on-Sea, England, with his wife and three children.

Series creator:

David Salariya was born in Dundee, Scotland, where he studied illustration and printmaking. He has illustrated a wide range of books and has created many new series of books for publishers in the UK and overseas. In 1989 he established The Salariya Book Company. He lives in Brighton, England, with his wife, the illustrator Shirley Willis, and their son.

Editors:

Stephen Haynes
Caroline Coleman

Published in Great Britain in MMXIV by
Book House, an imprint of
The Salariya Book Company Ltd
25 Marlborough Place, Brighton, BNI IUB
www.salariya.com
www.book-house.co.uk

ISBN 978-1-909645-79-0

SALARIYA

A CIP Catalogue record for this book is available from the British Library.

Printed and bound in China.
Printed on paper from sustainable sources.

PAPER FROM
SUSTAINABLE
FORESTS

Visit our website at **www.book-house.co.uk** or **www.salariya.com** for free electronic versions of:
You Wouldn't Want to be an Egyptian Mummy!
You Wouldn't Want to be a Roman Gladiator!
Avoid Joining Shackleton's Polar Expedition!
Avoid Sailing on a 19th-Century Whaling Ship!

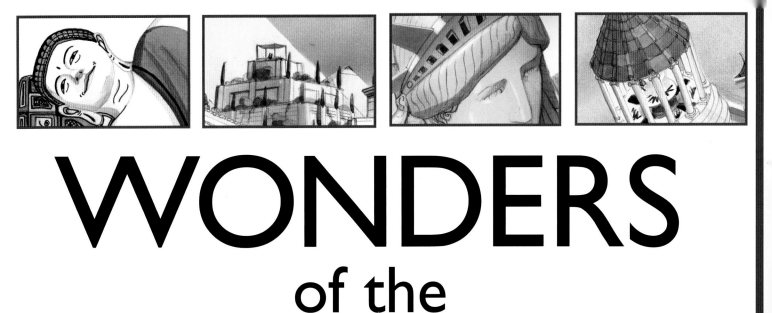

WONDERS
of the
WORLD

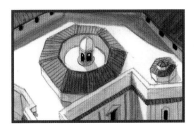

Written and illustrated by
MARK BERGIN

Created and designed by
DAVID SALARIYA

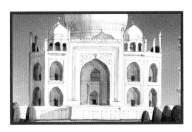

BOOK HOUSE
a SALARIYA imprint

Contents

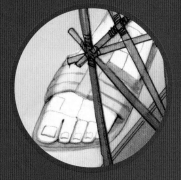
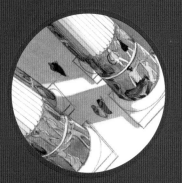
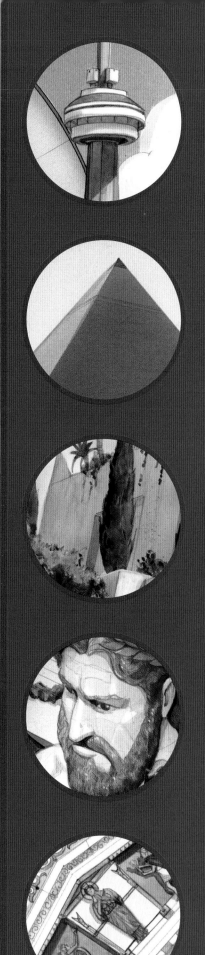

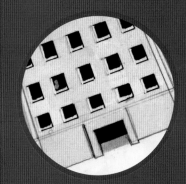

Ancient and modern wonders

The 'Wonders of the Ancient World' were first listed over 2,000 years ago.

The number of wonders was limited to seven because the number seven was thought to have mystical or religious meaning.

Statue of Zeus

Mausoleum of Halicarnassus

Temple of Artemis

The sites of the Seven Wonders of the Ancient World.

Colossus of Rhodes

Pharos of Alexandria

Hanging Gardens of Babylon

Pyramids of Giza

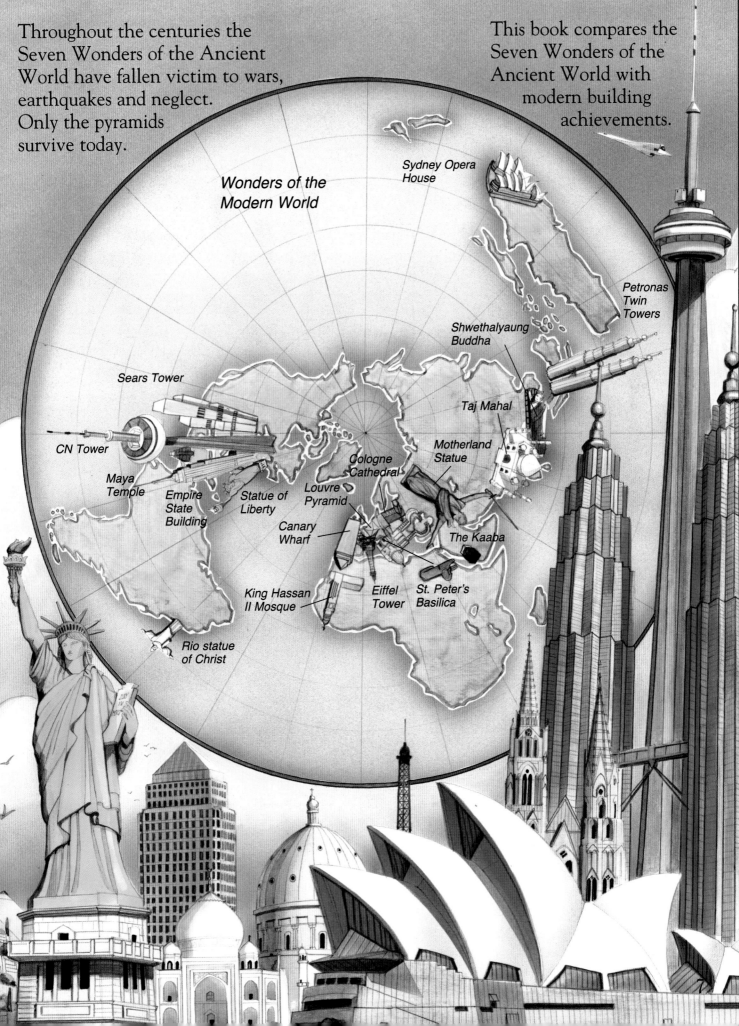

Throughout the centuries the Seven Wonders of the Ancient World have fallen victim to wars, earthquakes and neglect. Only the pyramids survive today.

This book compares the Seven Wonders of the Ancient World with modern building achievements.

Wonders of the Modern World

Sydney Opera House

Shwethalyaung Buddha

Petronas Twin Towers

Sears Tower

Taj Mahal

CN Tower

Motherland Statue

Maya Temple

Empire State Building

Statue of Liberty

Louvre Pyramid

Cologne Cathedral

Canary Wharf

The Kaaba

King Hassan II Mosque

Eiffel Tower

St. Peter's Basilica

Rio statue of Christ

Pyramids of Giza

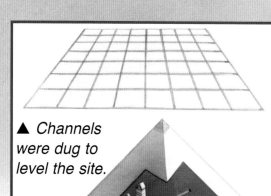

▲ Channels were dug to level the site.

▶ The grand gallery and the burial chambers.

The Pyramids at Giza were built over 5,000 years ago, as tombs for the **pharaohs** of ancient Egypt. They are the oldest of the Seven Wonders of the World. Each pyramid was intended to protect a pharaoh's body forever.

▶ Nile riverboats carried **limestone** from the quarries of Aswan and Tura to the site of the great pyramids.

Access ramps were built against each face of the pyramid. They were extended as the pyramid grew higher.

9

The dead pharaoh is pictured here making his last journey across the Nile to the river's west bank and the land of the dead.

Pyramid of Menkaure (Mycerinus)

Valley temple

Mourners

Pharaoh's state-boat

Death of the pharaoh

▼ A state-boat like the one below was found buried at the bottom of the pyramid of Khufu. It was made of cedar wood.

Pyramid of Khafre (Chephren)

▶ This Jaguar temple dated AD 600–900 was built by the Mayans of Cental America.

▼ This pyramid at the Louvre, France, was built in 1988.

Pyramid of Khufu (Cheops)

Hanging Gardens of Babylon

These exotic terraced gardens were built in the 9th century BC (in modern Iraq). The gardens, thought to have been built for King Nebuchadnezzar, rose up out of the desert. A system of hidden pipes brought water from the nearby River Euphrates up to its **terraces** of trees, plants and aromatic flowers.

▲ The garden of the Taj Mahal, India, was laid out in a geometric design.

▼ The Ryoanji garden in Kyoto, Japan, symbolises Zen Buddhist thought.

▲ Kublai Khan's Chinese palace gardens included animals and a lake with fish.

▲ In the 18th century, England's gardens became less formal and more natural.

Ziggurat

◄ *The Palace of Versailles in France, built by Louis XIV, has an abundance of beautiful gardens, ornamental lakes, fountains and statues.*

Hanging Gardens of Babylon

▼ *King Nebuchadnezzar's city of Babylon was one of the wealthiest cities in the ancient world.*

13

Temple of Zeus

Sheets of ivory and gold were hung on an iron frame.

The ancient Greek temple of Zeus, king of the gods, at Olympia, was seen as an object of perfection and power. Some say that the great statue was taken to Constantinople (modern Istanbul), where it was destroyed by fire.

Zeus's eyes were made from precious gemstones.

Statue of Nike, the winged goddess of victory.

Zeus's staff is topped with an eagle, a symbol of power.

Burning incense

Offerings to Zeus

Statue of Zeus

It took Phidias, the sculptor, 22 years to build the colossal statue of Zeus. The body was carved from ivory and the hair, beard and drapery were made from sheets of gold.

▼ *Reconstruction of the temple of Zeus at Olympia.*

▼ *Millions of Muslims make an annual pilgrimage to Mecca, Islam's holy city. The* **Kaaba** *stands in the central courtyard of the* **mosque**.

Kaaba

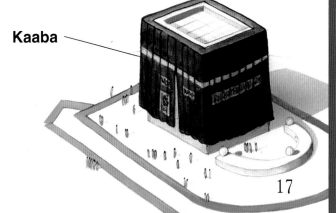

17

Decorated friezes, showing gods, heroes and mythical beasts.

In the temple stood a statue of Artemis, the Greek goddess of hunting and fertility, made of gold, silver and gems.

Each end of the temple had a carved marble pediment (triangular panel) showing Zeus, Artemis, Poseidon and Hera receiving **offerings** and **sacrifices**.

18

Temple of Artemis

The temple of Artemis at Ephesus in Turkey was rebuilt by Alexander the Great. This took 120 years, as it was one of the largest temples of its time.

▲ *This statue of Buddha, dating from the 10th century BC, was found in Burma (Myanmar) in 1881.*

▶ *The mosque of King Hassan II in Morocco is one of the largest mosques ever built. It holds up to 100,000 worshippers.*

▲ *St Peter's **Basilica** in Rome, Italy, was built between 1506 and 1626, on the site of the tomb of Peter the Apostle. It was the largest church in the world until 1989.*

19

▲In 1974, farmers digging a well near the Chinese city of Xian discovered life-size terracotta warriors, part of an army guarding the tomb of the first Emperor, Qin Shi Huang.

Mausoleum of Halicarnassus

This vast monument was built in Halicarnassus (modern Turkey) in memory of King Mausolus of Caria in 354 BC.

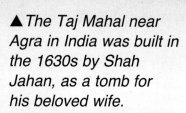

▲The Taj Mahal near Agra in India was built in the 1630s by Shah Jahan, as a tomb for his beloved wife.

Building King Mausolus' **tomb** took ten years and thousands of workers. Pythius, the **architect** who built the temple above the tomb, and Scopas, who made its **frieze** and many statues, were two of the best craftsmen in Greece. **Mausoleum**, the modern word for a large and splendid tomb, comes from the name of this ancient king.

▶ Marble statue of Mausolus and Artemisia.

Pyramid-like roof

Temple

Tomb of Mausolus

Colossus of Rhodes

The colossal statue of Helios the sun god was built in 300 BC. It stood in Rhodes' main harbour and was around 37 m in height.

▼ Giant statues through time: Egypt's **Sphinx**, America's Statue of Liberty, Brazil's statue of Christ and the tallest of all, Russia's Motherland.

The **Colossus** was destroyed about 70 years later, in 226 BC, when an earthquake toppled it into the sea.

Observation windows

Liberty's face is 3 m wide.

▶ Over 300 sheets of copper, about 3 mm thick, cover the statue.

Statue of Liberty

Liberty holds a tablet inscribed with the date when America declared its independence from Britain.

The spikes on Liberty's crown represent the seven seas and continents of the world.

From torch to toe, Liberty is 47 m high and weighs 185 tonnes.

The stone pedestal is roughly as high as the statue.

The Statue of Liberty overlooks Manhattan Island, New York. It was built over a hundred years ago to commemorate the centenary of American independence from Britain.

▶ The sculpture is hollow. It is constructed from sheets of shaped copper, fixed to a metal 'skeleton' that was designed by Gustave Eiffel who built the Eiffel Tower in Paris.

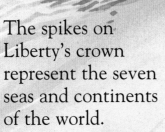

Pharos of Alexandria

The lighthouse of the city of Alexandria, Egypt, stood on the island of **Pharos**. At its summit a beacon burned day and night. The light was so bright it could be seen 50 km out to sea.

The Pharos was completed around 280 BC. An earthquake finally destroyed it in the 13th century.

Fire

Mirror

Spiral ramp

▼ Roman coins show what the Pharos looked like.

▶ Ship heading out of port.

The lighthouse was built in three stages of vaulted masonry. A large concave mirror reflected and intensified the light of the flaming beacon in the top storey.

The Pharos of Alexandria took 20 years to build.

Greek god
Helios

Concave
mirror to
reflect light

Tall towers

Today's skylines are dominated by tall towers. In 1889, the Eiffel Tower in Paris was the world's tallest structure. Today, it is the Burj Khalifa in Dubai at 829.8 m high.

Causeway to city of Alexandria

The high walled platform offered protection from the sea.

Empire State (380 m)

Sears Tower (527 m)

CN Tower (446 m)

Petronas Towers (452 m)

Eiffel Tower (324 m)

Useful words

Architect
Designer of buildings.

Basilica
A Christian church with a broad centre, side aisles and a dome.

Colossus
A very large statue. The Colossus of Rhodes was over 20 times life size.

Frieze
Horizontal band of decoration running around a building.

Kaaba
The cuboid building at the centre of Islam's most sacred mosque, Al-Masjid al-Haram, in Mecca.

Limestone
White stone which is easy to carve. The Egyptian pyramids were built of limestone and granite.

Mausoleum
The tomb of King Mausolus. It now means any large tomb.

Mosque
A Muslim place of worship.

Offerings
Gifts of food or artefacts offered to the gods.

Pharaoh
The title of an Egyptian king. It comes from two Egyptian words 'per o', meaning 'great house'.

Pharos
The island on which the lighthouse at Alexandria stood.

'Pharos' still means 'lighthouse' in many languages.

Sacrifices
Offerings to gods of food, wine or animals.

Sphinx
Ancient Egyptian form of the sun god. Has the body of a lion and the head of the pharaoh.

Terrace
Raised platform for standing, walking, or growing things.

Tomb
Elaborate building with a grave at its centre.

Ziggurat
Type of stepped pyramid structure in ancient Mesopotamia (modern Iraq).

Wonders of the World facts

▲The Sydney Opera House in Australia is made up of a series of sail-like roofs.

The Hanging Gardens of Babylon in Iraq are estimated to have been 90 m high.

The Statue of Zeus at Olympia is said to have been 12 m high.

The Temple of Artemis was one of the largest temples of its time – possibly 113 m long and 52 m wide.

The Mausoleum of Halicarnassus towered to a height of 45 m.

Cologne Cathedral in Germany took two hundred years to complete. The new towers made in the 1860s are 158 m tall.

The Basilica of St Peter's in Rome, Italy, was built between 1506 and 1626. Its huge dome rises to a height of over 138 m and until 1989 it was the largest church in the world.

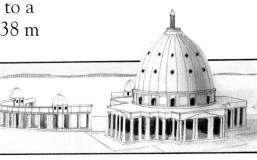

The Eiffel Tower, Paris, reaches a height of 302 m. It was the world's tallest structure until 1930.

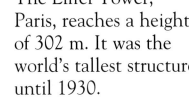

◀A modern pyramid stands in front of the Louvre Museum, Paris.

The Empire State building in Manhattan, the world's tallest building in 1930, took just over a year to build.

The Shard, in London, is Britain's tallest building at 310 m high.

The largest of the pyramids at Giza is still the world's largest stone structure.

▲The Basilica of Our Lady of Peace on the Ivory Coast, Africa, is 160 m high and 195 m long.

The Burj Khalifa in Dubai is the tallest man-made structure in the world, at an astonishing 829.8 m.

Index